KENYA & UGANDA

by
Dr. Benjamin E. Thomas

AROUND   THE   WORLD   PROGRAM

Prepared with the co-operation of the
American Geographical Society

EAST AFRICA HAS OFTEN BEEN DESCRIBED as a hot, steaming jungle full of wild animals and naked savages. Actually, jungles are hard to find there; vast plateaux with temperate climates and lofty mountains with snow-covered crests are more typical. Wild animals there are in abundance, but most of them live in open grasslands with scattered trees. And the people are a varied lot: Europeans, Asians and Africans. Even among the scores of African tribes the differences in dress, physical appearance, language and customs are as great as the differences between Englishmen and Hungarian gypsies or between Swedes and Italians.

From the Coast to the Congo

KENYA, WITH A POPULATION of 8.6 million, and Uganda, with about 7.2 million, extend from the Indian Ocean across the East African plateau to immense Lake Victoria and the other bodies of water that form the sources of the River Nile. The combined area of the two countries, 318,941 square miles, is approximately the size of France plus West Germany in Europe, or of the two states of Texas and Louisiana in the United States. In journeying westward from the coast one crosses four quite different kinds of country.

3

Africans sometimes harvest corn (maize) and then tie it in trees where it can dry and be protected from animals at the same time. Corn, made into *posho,* a form of porridge, is a staple food among many peoples of Kenya and Uganda.

Northern Kenya is a semi-desert area with many nomadic tribes. Camels are often used for swift raids upon rival tribes or for moving the family to a new grazing area.

14.   SOMALI NOMADS IN NORTHERN KENYA

A twenty-mile-wide strip along the coast is low-lying, hot and plentifully supplied with rain. For more than 2,000 years this damp coast has been visited by Indian, Persian and Arab seamen, whose small sailing vessels were propelled by the monsoon winds, which blow south-westward for a season and then reverse and blow north-eastward.

4

Beyond this coastal strip begins the Nyika, meaning "wilderness" in the local Swahili language. This barren scrubland of scattered acacia trees is plagued with long periods of drought, especially in the north, as well as with tsetse flies that spread the dreaded African sleeping sickness. Nevertheless, Arab slavers used to venture into it and beyond in search of captives. The slaves were compelled to carry ivory tusks to the coast and then both men and ivory were sold in the markets of Mombasa or Zanzibar. When a railway was built, danger from man-eating lions added another chapter to the history of toil and misery in the Nyika.

Westward the land rises gradually until, about 350 miles inland, it reaches elevations of 5,000 to 7,000 feet, with mountains that rise much higher. This country is known as the Highlands. It has ample rainfall, is cool rather than hot, and is generally free from both the malaria of the coast and the sleeping sickness of the wilderness. Mount Kenya, rising to 17,058 feet, and the great Rift Valley provide spectacular scenery, and the fertile soil and temperate climate offer

15.   MOTOR DRIVE ALONG THE SEA FRONT AT MOMBASA, KENYA

Mombasa and the other coastal towns of Kenya have the blue waters of the Indian Ocean for bathing. There are many coral islands, as well as sandy beaches fringed by palm trees.

5

attractions for European farmers. The main city, Nairobi, with 330,000 people, is the largest in East Africa.

Farther west lies Uganda, which is again different. Much of it is plateau country with lush vegetation and blue lakes. Many parts of this region are inhabited by comparatively prosperous African farmers who derive their income mainly from cash crops such as cotton and coffee. There are no European settlers.

Locally made baskets as well as imported ones and metal wares are offered for sale in the market behind the mosque in Nairobi. Much of the small retail trade in Kenya and Uganda is carried on by Asians.

Safari Means Journey

THE ARAB SAILORS and European traders of past centuries commonly learned the language of the coastal or Swahili people, and through them it spread along the coast and inland. Each African people, of course, has its own language, but Swahili, an African Bantu language, is easy to learn, and it now serves as a *lingua franca* throughout eastern Africa, from southern Arabia to Durban in the Union of South Africa, and inland across Uganda to the Republic of the Congo.

A few Swahili words have spread even to Europe and America by way of films and stories. Many American and British people know that *bwana* means master, a *safari* is a journey and *simba* is a lion.

Bark from wattle trees is a major product of Kenya. After the strips are removed from trees they are tied in bundles and taken by bicycle or truck to local markets. About 5,000 tons of bark are converted each year into wattle extract.

21.   STRIPPING BARK FOR USE IN TANNING

Tropical, Sub-tropical and Temperate

WITH ALTITUDES VARYING from sea level to several thousand feet, climatic conditions are such that a great variety of tropical, sub-tropical, and temperate crops can be grown. In Kenya, at low altitudes along the coast, the cultivated land is mostly in corn, sisal, sugar, coconuts and cotton. In the Highlands and Nyanza Province the chief crops are corn, or maize (the staple food), coffee, wheat, wattle, sisal, tea and pyrethrum, the flowers of which yield a valuable insecticide. Kenya is the largest producer of tea in Africa, and the world's largest producer of pyrethrum. Livestock and such other crops as peanuts, beans and potatoes are also raised in many places.

In the warm and humid areas near Lake Victoria in Uganda one often sees groves of banana plants with manioc and vegetables, and a

7

great deal of cotton is grown. Less humid areas are devoted to sorghum, or millet which must be pounded into flour before using. Uganda is the largest coffee producer in the British Commonwealth. Other cash crops include tea, tobacco, peanuts and sugar.

The Farm Homestead

THE FARMS OF MOST EAST AFRICANS are small gardens, or *shambas*. Usually a man has several wives. In some tribes, each of them has a separate hut for herself and her children, and the several huts and small grain storehouses are enclosed by a hedge or fence. In other tribes, the farmstead has a main house for the man and his senior wife, huts for girls, huts for boys and goats together, and perhaps additional huts for junior wives, grandparents and guests. The styles and arrangements vary from tribe to tribe.

The women generally tend the shambas, carry water and prepare the meals, leaving the men free to serve as warriors, to look after the cattle, to work elsewhere, or to loaf and visit their friends. Under the circumstances, an extra wife or two comes in handy to share the work.

High-quality coffee has been a major product of European farms in Kenya for many years and is now raised by Africans as well. After picking, the coffee berries must be dried and roasted. More than 43,000 tons are exported each year.

11. DRYING COFFEE ON A KENYA FARM

African farmers near the towns of Kenya supply oranges, lemons, peppers and a variety of other fruits and vegetables for sale in the daily markets to meet the varied tastes of Europeans, Asians and Africans. Both women and men bargain with enthusiasm.

Marriage Insurance

AMONG MOST OF THE EAST AFRICAN PEOPLES a "bride price" of cattle, goats, or other form of wealth must be paid by the bridegroom and his family to the family of the bride. This "marriage insurance" serves as a stabilizing influence, for it makes the bridegroom and his family consider the matter seriously before parting with the payment. And the family of the bride will later exert pressure to make

9

Women play a large part in African markets with their beans, millet, or vegetables displayed for sale. Bargaining over prices, paying visits to friends, and exchanging news are also enjoyed as social pastimes.

22.   AFRICAN MARKET IN SOROTI, UGANDA

the marriage a success, because the animals must be returned if the bride is not satisfactory.

Family ties are strong and there is usually a well-developed loyalty to the clan, or group of families. In a few places, each clan has a "totem", usually a plant or animal, which identifies the clan and to which special rites are devoted. Members of the clan are prohibited from eating the totem plant or animal.

The spread of Christianity is decreasing the number of families with plural wives, but in the rural regions they and the bride price are normal and widespread customs. Among detribalized Africans in the towns both customs are passing out of use.

Schools and Hospitals

IN BOTH KENYA AND UGANDA almost three-quarters of the children now attend primary schools run by the government. The larger towns have government-supported elementary and high schools, and there are several technical and trade schools.

The former strict racial division of education—for European, Asian, or African—has started to yield to a multi-racial approach. Privately supported Asian schools, especially those of the Ismaili Moslem sect, have admitted a few Africans in both Kenya and Uganda. Some state schools in Uganda admit qualified students of all races. And both Makerere College and the University College now have African, Asian and European students.

The larger towns of East Africa have hospitals; the smaller ones have only dispensaries with visiting doctors. Although great progress has been made in curbing plagues such as malaria and sleeping sickness, most Africans in remote areas live out their lives without ever seeing a doctor or a dentist and depend upon tribal faith and traditional medicines and ceremonies to cure their ills.

A War Against Flies

THE TSETSE FLY, not much different in appearance from a small house fly, spreads sleeping sickness among humans and another

Chief Arap Tengeche of Kenya poses outside his house with his wife and one of his children. Many Africans in responsible positions have adopted European clothing and housing, and there is a demand all over East Africa for European-style education.

disease, nagana, among domestic animals. Wild animals, such as antelopes, carry the disease without being affected by it. The flies live in bushes and trees and, by biting first one victim and then another, transmit diseases to man and his susceptible domestic animals.

Fortunately, the fly finds the Kenya Highlands too cool. And the

Makerere College, at Kampala, Uganda, is at the apex of East African education. Outstanding students from Kenya, Uganda, and Tanzania take instruction and examinations for degrees awarded by the University of London.

The home of a planter in Kenya. European farms often have hundreds of acres with dozens of African workers, or "squatters", who plant and harvest crops or tend animals in exchange for small wages and a plot of ground for a hut and garden.

5.   MAIN HALL AT MAKERERE COLLEGE

drier parts of Kenya and Uganda will not support enough brush to provide a home for it. Also, new wonder drugs can cure sleeping sickness in people if they are treated promptly and frequently. But coping with the animal disease is still a major problem in places where the fly lives.

Vaccination of cattle is expensive and difficult. The killing of wild animals to exterminate the carriers of the disease is a drastic and probably unjustifiable course. Another method is to clear brush to eliminate the flies from pasturelands and to form brush-free barriers between infected and fly-free regions. Fly traps and fly collectors can clear fields, and cattle movements can be controlled to prevent the

spread of flies to disease-free areas. In places, by a combination of these methods, flies have been eliminated enough to permit grazing, but it is often hard to maintain the battle lines.

The tsetse fly has caused much misery in tropical Africa. Because it was impossible to use horses, donkeys, or other animals, the old foot safari was often the only means of transport. And there are still vast areas where people cannot keep animals for milk, meat, farm work, or transport, nor make use of rich pasturelands, because of this fly.

The Hindu Temple in Mombasa has a striking and unusual tower and an intricate design for arches, pillars and roof. Many Asian homes have stained-glass windows and fancy ironwork in grills and railings.

These are homes for workers in Mombasa's docks and industries. The Changamwe housing estate, when completed, will accommodate about 3,700 workers in four-room houses. Most of the houses are available for purchase by tenants.

Mombasa: "Island of War"

MOMBASA, TOWARDS THE SOUTH END of Kenya's coastline, is that country's chief port and second city in size, and has played an important part in the history of the coast for as long as written records have been kept. It is believed to date back to long before the birth of

Christ. Vasco da Gama stopped there in 1498 on his famous voyage around Africa to India. The Portuguese and Arabs struggled over it from 1500 to 1784, and it was besieged and changed hands so many times that it justly earned the name "Island of War".

Fort Jesus, built by the Portuguese in 1592–95, when Mombasa was the capital of the Portuguese territories in East Africa, is still a massive and impressive landmark. The fort stands at the entrance of Mombasa's Old Port, which is now used by Arab dhows and other small craft. Nearby are the old buildings and narrow streets of the Arab and Indian quarters of the city.

From December to April the ocean-going dhows, following the monsoon winds, arrive at the Old Port, and the quarter takes on new life. Swarthy and bearded Arab seamen, dressed in turbans, loose-fitting blouses and baggy trousers, with long knives at their belts, swagger down the streets in the typical fashion of sailors on shore leave. The fleet remains for many weeks, until the monsoon from the south-west is ready to blow the ships back to Arabia with their cargoes of coconuts, mangrove poles and ivory.

19.   ELEPHANT TUSK PILLARS ON KILINDINI ROAD IN MOMBASA

Kilindini Road is a major thoroughfare of Mombasa with shops, hotels and banks. The arch of elephant tusks reminds the visitor of the heritage of African big game and the traditional trade in ivory.

15

1862 – FIRST EUROPEANS, J.H. SPEKE AND J.A. GRANT, ENTER UGANDA.

DESCRIPTION OF KENYA C WRITTEN BY A GREEK FRO ALEXANDRIA, EGYPT ABOU TIME OF CHRIST.

WHITE NILE

1872 – SIR SAMUEL BAKER SUPPRESSED SLAVERY, ATTACHED PART OF UGANDA TO SUDAN UNTIL 1889.

HAMITIC TRIBES MIGRATED INTO KENYA – UGANDA REGION 3000 – 4000 YEARS AGO FROM NORTHEAST.

UGANDA

L. KYOGA

OWEN FALLS DA AND HYDROELE PLANT BUILT IN

L. ALBERT

REPUBLIC

N

• KASESE

• JINJA

• KAMPALA

• ENTEBBE

L. EDWARD

MBARARA •

LAKE VICTORIA

OF THE

KABALE •

FROM 1879, UPON ESTABLISHMENT OF FRENCH MISSION, STARTED THE RIVALRY OF ISLAM CATHOLICISM AND PROTESTANTISM.

CONGO

RWANDA

BURUNDI

1875, HENRY M. STANLEY VISITED UGANDA URGED DEVELOPMENT OF COUNTRY.

L. TANGANYIKA

ETHIOPIA

LAKE RUDOLF

WARLIKE MASAI MIGRATED FROM NORTH DURING 18TH CENTURY.

MOYALE

1941 – WORLD WAR II KENYA FORCES FOUGHT IN ETHIOPIA AND BURMA,

REPUBLIC

1952 – 56 MAU-MAU TERROR HASTENED FORMATION OF REPUBLIC.

KENYA

5 – BISHOP HANNINGTON RDERED IN UGANDA WHEN ARED AS SUPPOSED CONQUEROR.

MARSABIT •

WAJIR •

1887– SULTAN BARGHASH OF ZANZIBAR GRANTED CONCESSION TO BRITISH OVER COAST OF KENYA.

SOMALI

1883 – JOSEPH THOMSON FIRST EUROPEAN TO TRAVERSE THE MASAI COUNTRY.

ITALE

1896 – RAILWAY FROM MOMBASA TO KISUMU TO KAMPALA BEGUN. RAILWAY SPELLED END OF SLAVERY BY ELIMINATING HUMAN CARRIERS BY CARAVAN.

• MERU

UMU •

1964– KENYA FORMS REPUBLIC UNDER PRESIDENT JOMO KENYATTA.

• BURA

TANA

• NAIROBI

14-18 WORLD WAR I – ENYA FORCES HELPED EFEAT TROOPS FROM ERMAN EAST AFRICA.

1698-1784 ARABS WON COAST AND MOMBASA FROM PORTUGUESE

• WITU

OCEAN

• MALINDI

Historical Events
of
KENYA and UGANDA

MOMBASA •

TANZANIA

INDIAN

1498 – VASCO DA GAMA VISITED KENYA COAST ON WAY TO INDIA. 1505 – PORTUGUESE OCCUPY MOMBASA.

Many of the dhows are built by hand at the smaller ports of the Kenya coast. The ships are almost immortal, for as each timber becomes infirm it is replaced by a new sound one.

Between Mombasa Island and the mainland lies a fine bay, called Kilindini, which means "deep waters" in Swahili. Nearby a big oil refinery, which can process 2 million tons of crude oil a year, has been built, together with a tanker berth and an oil storage terminal. The oil comes from Arabia. This port, provided with piers and railways, has become the busiest between Aden and South Africa, the main imports being manufactured goods, fuels, motor vehicles, machinery and parts, fabrics and sugar, and the main exports cotton, coffee, tea, sisal, copper and alloys, wattle bark extract and hides and skins. The city of Mombasa has also grown tremendously since World War II, to 180,000 people, who take great pride in their many modern stores, hotels and offices.

North of Mombasa are the two small ports of Lamu and Malindi. Lamu has ancient Persian ruins as well as Arab commercial houses, and a flourishing dhow-building industry. Until recently, remarkable vessels called *M'tepes* were built here of planks sewn together, with a prow like the head of a camel, whose design, it is claimed, had not changed for 2,000 years. Malindi has become a seaside resort with beach houses and hotels that appeal to European holiday-seekers.

The fishing dhows of Lake Victoria are smaller replicas of the famous sea-going Arab dhows which ply between East Africa and Arabia. Lake fish are sent to many parts of Kenya and Uganda.

9.   FISHING DHOWS ON LAKE VICTORIA

The Scramble for East Africa

AFTER THE EXPULSION of the Portuguese in 1784 the most powerful force on the east coast of Africa was the Sultan of Muscat from Arabia. The island of Zanzibar, about 150 miles south of Mombasa, was then the Arab capital of East Africa. In 1832 Sultan Seyyid Said moved his headquarters from Muscat to Zanzibar, in order to oversee more effectively the profitable slave traffic that flowed through Zanzibar from the whole of eastern Africa.

In Great Britain, however, public opinion was rising against the slave trade. Sultan Seyyid Said was eventually persuaded to curtail the slave traffic in exchange for a British guarantee of Zanzibar's independence. Thus began the alliance between Britain and Zanzibar— and British influence in East Africa, which has continued to the present.

By 1887 threats of French and German domination of East Africa led the rulers of Zanzibar to seek even closer ties with Britain. Sultan Barghash offered Sir William Mackinnon, chairman of the British India line, control of the customs and administration of all the dominions of Zanzibar with the exceptions of Zanzibar and Pemba Islands; but the

Cyanite, a native silicate of aluminum, is dug from the hill in the background and hauled to the plant for processing at a mine near Taveta, Kenya. The plant converts the cyanite to mullite, most of which is exported, while some is used for making mullite bricks.

British Foreign Office refused to support the plan. Instead, a private concern, the Imperial British East Africa Company, was established to develop trade.

A few years later the pressures existing in Britain for further intervention overcame the government's reluctance to take on further responsibilities in East Africa. The pressures came from anti-slavery forces which wanted Britain to stop the slave trade altogether; from imperialists who were alarmed at new German treaties with African chiefs on the mainland opposite Zanzibar; and from groups who wanted protection for missionaries in Uganda. A British protectorate over Zanzibar, Kenya and Uganda, it seemed, would be the answer. A series of treaties signed between 1890 and 1896 acknowledged British interests in these areas. Germany gained control of German East Africa (later known as Tanganyika, and now part of Tanzania), opposite Zanzibar and south of Kenya.

The Lunatic Line

IN ORDER TO CRUSH the slave trade in the interior, establish and maintain British order and justice, and develop the trade of productive Uganda, a railway from Mombasa on the coast to Lake Victoria was needed. Interior Kenya at that time was regarded as merely a passageway to Uganda, and of no particular value otherwise.

Construction on the railway started in 1896, despite powerful opposition in Britain. From the first the project ran into all sorts of difficulties. Manual workers were so scarce that thousands of coolies had to be imported from India, along with the Indian foods they required. There were strikes in England that held up materials. Natural obstacles such as wide expanses without surface water, the great Rift Valley and high mountains created other problems. At one point, between Nairobi and Uganda, the line climbed to an altitude of 9,150 feet. But the most terrifying obstacle was the lions.

At Tsavo, 130 miles from Mombasa, in December, 1898, work was delayed for three weeks by man-eating lions. The crews went hunting for sport and for food, and the antelopes, gazelles, zebras and other animals upon which lions normally prey soon fled to other parts. The lions, deprived of their usual fare, turned to stalking and eating the railway workers. One night a European waiting in a railway car with rifle in hand to shoot the marauders was seized by a lion which had come in by the door. The man-eaters carried off twenty-eight Indians and scores of Africans before they were finally tracked down and shot.

The railway, 577 miles long, finally reached Lake Victoria in 1901.

A Diet of Blood and Milk

As the visitor approaches the Highlands of southern Kenya, he comes into the land of the Masai. In the days when the railway was being built the Masai warriors, equipped with spears and shields, were famous for their arrogance and fearlessness.

The main food of the Masai, wandering with their herds of cattle in search of pasture, was a nourishing drink of blood and milk, both obtained from the cattle. Masai boys were separated from the girls and given strenuous training as warriors. One of the marks of manhood was to kill a lion with a spear. It was considered great sport to raid nearby tribes. The men, tall, lean and muscular, joined together in companies and regiments with great zest for testing their military tactics upon available opponents.

The Masai's raiding and cattle stealing have now been curtailed, but the military traditions, the prestige connected with owning cattle, and other customs, all persist. Their huts, built of an archwork of branches plastered over the top with mud for a roof, are little more than rudimentary shelters from rain and sun. Few of the Masai have abandoned the old ways for new ones.

Each African tribe has its rhythmic dances, accompanied by drums and musical instruments, to celebrate important occasions, to please the native gods, to provide social relaxation, or to entertain important visitors.

10. DANCERS AT WITU IN EASTERN KENYA

The Masai of Kenya and Tanzania retain their ancient customs and their close attachment to their cattle. At first they refused to sell cattle, but the Masai will now sell part of their herds, as at this yearly market.

Kamba Land

JUST EAST OF THE HIGHLANDS farther north are the Kamba people. The early trails to interior Kenya passed through Kamba country and avoided Masai land as much as possible. The Kamba kept cattle and raised crops on their rather barren hills. They were willing to barter food for knives and cloth and allowed traders to pass through their territory. When they were so disposed, of course, they sent forth military expeditions against the Masai and often won local engagements, and sometimes made trouble for strangers; but most of the time they looked after their cattle, their *shambas* and their trading.

The Kamba have the reputation of being high-spirited and are famed for their high violent jumps and somersaults in their traditional dances. They have been one of the most helpful people to the British. Many have become soldiers in the army, and selected six-

In a drive against witchcraft and terrorism in the Kamba tribe, the Kenya government collected magic charms and other implements of witchcraft for destruction by burning at a ceremony at Kinau. Four hundred witches gathered at Kinau and renounced their calling.

An Orma family in a village near Garsen in the Tana River District of Kenya. The nomadic Orma people, also known as the Galla, are a mixture of Hamitic and Negroid strains, as are many of the other tribes of north-eastern Kenya.

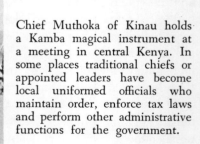

Chief Muthoka of Kinau holds a Kamba magical instrument at a meeting in central Kenya. In some places traditional chiefs or appointed leaders have become local uniformed officials who maintain order, enforce tax laws and perform other administrative functions for the government.

The Kamba tribe of Kenya has traditionally made carved figures of wood. They sell woodcarvings all over East Africa, and send some abroad. Other tribes have also started making carvings for sale to tourists.

1. WOODCARVINGS FOR SALE AT KAMPALA

footers serve in the police force. The Kamba also work as drivers of motor vehicles, as manual workers and in other unskilled and skilled jobs. Unlike the Masai, many now attend elementary schools and wear European-type clothing.

Big Game Capital

WHERE THE RAILWAY paused in May of 1899 at a watering place, while workshops were constructed and equipment assembled for the ascent of the hills along the eastern edge of the Rift Valley, a village sprouted. It was soon expanded by the shops of Indians who came from the coast to sell clothing and cooking utensils and imported foods to the railway employees. Before long an inland town was established—Nairobi.

Additional towns arose at other strategic spots, usually with In-

25

dians as the first tradesmen. Although most of the Indian coolies who built the railway returned to India, some stayed. And the railway was the means by which the Indian traders and their goods were brought to the interior. With great commercial skill and tenacity, the Indians increased the number, size and variety of their establishments, until now every interior town in both Kenya and Uganda has its Indian traders, some of them very wealthy. In Nairobi there are whole streets lined with Indian shops, although the largest concerns are generally European-owned.

Nairobi started as a railway camp with a few shops where Asians sold goods to the workers. This is the first Nairobi headquarters of the National Bank of India. Early buildings often had frames of wood with roofs and walls of corrugated iron.

3.   GOVERNMENT HOUSE IN NAIROBI

Government House, the residence of governors when Kenya was a colony and protectorate, has been the scene of important political meetings, as well as a focus of social life for public officials and many distinguished visitors.

The bright hues and modernistic styles of new apartments, stores and office buildings in Nairobi give the central area a European aspect. Numerous cars, traffic lights and parking meters add to the impression.

23.   AN ULTRA-MODERN BUILDING IN NAIROBI

Nairobi currently has more people, and more modern buildings and cars than any other place in East Africa. The population is 330,000, including about 24,000 Europeans, and 98,000 Asians. Cars are so numerous that despite new boulevards and parking meters, traffic jams and parking problems are severe.

Nairobi is famous as the headquarters for big game hunting. Each year many visitors fly in, engage a white hunter, and spend a few weeks on safari looking for elephants, rhinoceros, buffalo, bushbuck, or rarer animals such as the sable antelope. The number of people who prefer to use their skill in photographing rather than killing animals is increasing. Nairobi has a game park on the outskirts of the city where one can drive to see herds of zebra, hartebeest, wildebeest, giraffe and gazelles, as well as lions, roaming freely in their native habitat. Visitors are required to stay in their cars; they are usually ignored by the wild animals.

Nairobi has become a major hub of air traffic, with international routes that radiate northward to Europe, Sudan and Ethiopia, eastward to India, southward to Tanzania, Rhodesia and South Africa, and westward to Uganda, the Congo and Central and West Africa. Many tourists, businessmen and government officials go to Nairobi by

Nairobi is the capital of the new Republic of Kenya, as well as the administrative headquarters for the commission which regulates ports, currency, railways, roads and other services.

7.   PARLIAMENT BUILDING IN NAIROBI

long-distance airlines and then continue to their final destinations by the local lines which serve all the secondary cities.

The Rift Valley

THE SPECTACULAR RIFT VALLEY SYSTEM of East Africa is a series of great trenches with steep sides. In past geological ages the valleys were formed by the faulting (cracking) of the earth's crust and the gradual sinking of long, narrow blocks of rock. At the same time lava poured out from the cracks in many places and formed hills or mountains along the sides of the trenches.

The Rift Valley System starts in Israel and Jordan, about 3,000 miles north of Kenya. The River Jordan, the Dead Sea and the Red Sea all lie on the bottom of the trench. The valley continues across

Ethiopia and in northern Kenya splits into two branches. The Eastern Rift runs southward across Kenya and Tanzania. The Western Rift swings to western Uganda and then southward via lakes Albert, Edward, Kivu and Tanganyika.

Mile-high Farmers

ONCE THE RAILWAY was completed to Lake Victoria, an attempt was made to find additional traffic and revenue. Lord Delamere and

The Town Hall of Nairobi, built in 1957, is part of the City Square development of municipal and other public buildings. In the background is the Mitchell Cotts House. It has stores on the ground floor and offices, including the American Consulate, above.

As Nairobi grew from a trading post to the largest city of East Africa, buildings took on a more modern and permanent aspect. This shows the National Bank of India as it appeared in 1950 when Nairobi was granted a charter as a city.

29

Yearly feast of the balloons in Nairobi, an important event for raising charity funds. Balloons are sold and released. The one which travels the farthest from Nairobi brings to its owner the first prize, the second farthest, the second prize, and so on.

Delamere Avenue, its name commemorating the founder of European settlement and farming in the Kenya Highlands, is the main boulevard of Nairobi. A statue of Lord Delamere stands in a landscaped circle.

29.   DELAMERE AVENUE IN NAIROBI, KENYA

others thought that the Highlands could be settled by Europeans who would develop the country's resources. There were attempts at raising cattle, sheep, corn and wheat. Many failed because almost nothing was known of tropical plant and animal diseases, soils and climates. Strange cattle diseases, such as rinderpest and East Coast Fever, caused many losses. Sheep died mysteriously in some areas; the deaths were later traced to mineral deficiencies in the soil. Most disconcerting, there were two seasons of rainfall, instead of one as in Europe or South Africa.

But Lord Delamere persisted, in spite of all this, and he eventually proved that the Highlands were good farming country. He is regarded as the founder of European settlement in Kenya.

The British government intended to settle Europeans only on uninhabited lands, or lands that were little used by Africans. Native land units were set aside for Africans only. Other land in the Highlands was opened to European settlement only. Asians were restricted to the coast and to the towns. Hence, in the Kenya Highlands farmland was owned by either whites (Europeans) or Africans. Unfortunately, some of the land taken over by whites had been used for generations by Africans, who strongly resented the loss of it.

Nakuru, Agricultural Heart of the Highlands

THE FLOOR OF THE RIFT VALLEY was soon dotted with European farms and small towns once the railway was complete. Gradually, Nakuru outgrew the others. When a new rail line was built from Nakuru to Uganda the future of the town was assured. Nakuru's population of more than 38,000 people ranks it next to Nairobi among inland Kenya towns.

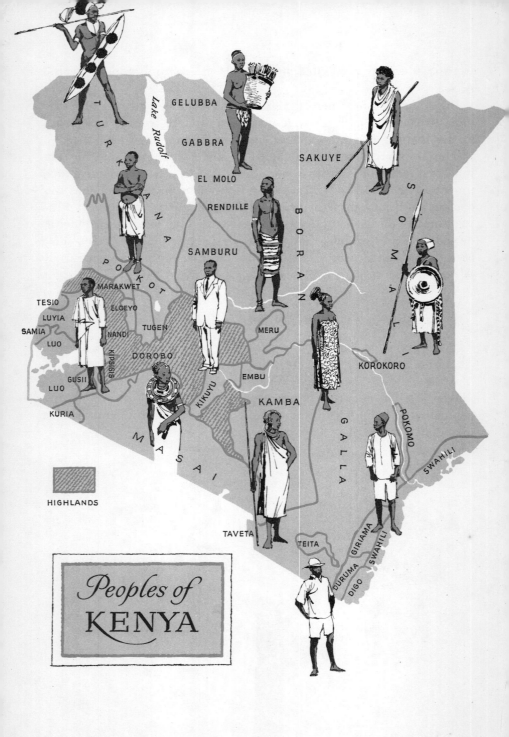

TURKANA

Lake Rudolf

GELUBBA

GABBRA

SAKUYE

EL MOLO

RENDILLE

BORAN

POKOT

SAMBURU

SOMALI

MARAKWET

TESIO

LUYIA

ELGEYO

SAMIA

NANDI

TUGEN

LUO

KIPSIGIS

GUSII

DOROBO

MERU

KOROKORO

LUO

EMBU

KURIA

KIKUYU

KAMBA

GALLA

POKOMO

MASAI

SWAHILI

HIGHLANDS

TAVETA

TEITA

DURUMA

GIRIAMA

SWAHILI

DIGO

Peoples of
KENYA

With wide streets, many new buildings, and a lake at its back door, Nakuru is a pleasant farming town and headquarters of the Kenya Farmers' Association. The elevation of 6,000 feet above sea level gives it a sub-tropical, rather than tropical, climate. Temperatures, like those of Nairobi, usually range in the 60s and low 70s and are comparable to those of coastal towns in southern California.

Africans from many tribes have settled in Nakuru and the city is proud of its African housing projects. Many Asian residences are of bright hues, and have fancy iron grillwork at the windows. Europeans live mostly in separate houses surrounded by lawns and flowers. Flamingos sometimes land on Lake Nakuru in such numbers that the surface has a pink shade rather than a blue one.

North and north-west of Nakuru, in the valley and on the plateau, are additional European farms. Eldoret and Kitale are market cities, smaller than Nakuru, but nonetheless new and pleasant urban spots with African, Asian and European elements.

The highway from Nakuru to Nairobi, and parts of the other main roads of Kenya, have tarmac (crushed stone and tar) surfaces. But most routes are of *murram*, a rocklike soil crust that is crushed and spread on the roads. Under the best conditions it packs down into a firm clay surface. In other cases, corrugations or "washboard" roads develop. Many roads are dusty in dry weather and soft and slippery in the rainy seasons. However, plans are under way for extensive new construction.

33

The fleet at Kisumu, Kenya, brings in large quantities of fish, especially ngege, which are caught in nets. Fish provide a staple food for the lakeside population, and dried fish are shipped to inland towns. At Lake George in western Uganda there are packing plants.

Africa's Largest Lake

WEST OF NAKURU one climbs up the western escarpment of the Rift Valley, crosses the Mau Summit at 8,322 feet above sea level, and then descends to Lake Victoria at 3,726 feet.

Lake Victoria is second only to North America's Lake Superior in size among the fresh-water lakes of the world. With an area of 26,828 square miles, Victoria is almost as large as Scotland. About 250 miles long, 150 miles wide, its deeply indented shoreline is shared by Kenya,

Uganda and Tanzania. When the lake was reported by explorers to be so tremendous and to be the long-sought source of the Nile as well, the claims were received with much reserve. Later the lake became better known and its value was understood.

Kisumu, at first known as Port Florence, was built to serve as a railway terminal and port on the lake. Then steamers were imported, piece by piece, over the railway and assembled at Kisumu for service on the lake. Taking a steamer across Lake Victoria is like going to sea; the shore soon disappears and for most of the journey no land is in sight.

Located on a shallow bay in which driftwood and refuse collected, Kisumu at first acquired an evil reputation as an unhealthy, malarial place. But medical services improved greatly, homes were built on

20.   FISHING FROM A POND MADE OF PAPYRUS STALKS, LAKE VICTORIA

Fish are trapped in Lake Victoria by enclosing a pond with papyrus stalks. The stalks are gradually moved into a small circle, and the fish can then be scooped out with a basket.

35

cooler sites on the nearby hills, and new buildings and parks were added to the town. It has become an attractive, healthy town with a population of more than 23,000. It is still the main port on Lake Victoria, but a direct rail line now runs from Nakuru to Uganda and only a part of the traffic goes by way of the lake and Kisumu.

After fish have been gathered from the ponds in Lake Victoria they are spread on rocks to dry and then divided among the families of the fishermen.

4.   A CATCH OF FISH FROM LAKE VICTORIA

The Nandi and the Luo Peoples

BETWEEN NAKURU AND KISUMU one crosses the lands of the Nandi and Luo peoples, among others. The Nandi, pastoralist like the Masai, are akin to them in physical type—a mixture of Hamitic and Negroid strains.

Many Nandi have adopted European dress and have turned to farming and the raising of improved cattle. The Nandi country, in contrast to the semi-arid Masai land, lies at elevations of 6,000 to 8,000 feet, with good soils and rainfall.

The humid and lower country around Kisumu is densely settled by

36

the Luo people, second in numbers only to the Kikuyu. The Luo were mostly farmers and fishermen at a subsistence level in the early days. But, like the Kikuyu, they learned quickly from Europeans and Asians and have become one of the leading African groups in farming, commerce and politics. There are more college-educated and influential Africans from the Luo and Kikuyu than from other Kenya peoples.

After sisal is cut, the fibrous strands are placed on racks to dry. Sisal is a major product of Kenya and adjoining Tanzania. About half of the total annual crop of more than 60,000 tons is exported, but there are also factories where sisal is made into bags and cordage for local use.

Washing coffee berries on a farm in Kenya. The Arabica coffee of the Kenya Highlands is of a superior quality and is raised on both European and African farms. Too expensive for the American market, most Kenya coffee is sold to Germany.

Mount Kenya and the Aberdares

THE HIGHEST PART OF KENYA is north of Nairobi. Mount Kenya, from which the colony took its name, is a gigantic snow-capped extinct volcano that rises to more than 17,000 feet. Below the snow are forests, and still lower, on the southern slopes, are the farms of the Kikuyu and the related Embu peoples. The Kikuyu lands extend southward to Nairobi and westward to the Aberdare Mountains.

The rugged and forested Aberdares have peaks over 12,000 feet high and the Kikuyu farms, here too, extend only part way up the slopes. Europeans were permitted to settle to the north and to the south-east of the Kikuyu, but in a few places where the Kikuyu lands were lightly

An African market often has an enclosure formed of permanent buildings—some are *dukas* or small general stores and others are occupied by butchers. On market days additional goods are displayed.

26.   MARKETPLACE IN AFRICAN VILLAGE

populated or temporarily unoccupied the government allowed land belonging to the Kikuyu to be taken by Europeans.

The European farms in the fertile Highlands raise fine cattle, wheat, corn and other products of temperate lands. There are also tropical plants such as coffee and pineapples, and sisal, which is used for twine and bags. But this part of Kenya is especially noted for big game hunting. The wily buffalo, wild African dogs and bushbuck live in the forests. Farmers have to guard their livestock from occasional leopards that prey upon goats or calves at night, and from wart hogs that spread disease among domestic pigs. Baboons, wart hogs and porcupines destroy crops.

Many European farmers supplement their incomes as "white hunters" for visitors who wish to photograph or shoot lions, elephants, zebra, or rhinoceros. There are hotels for tourists and hunters on the outskirts of the small towns, one of which, "Treetops", is built in the branches of a large tree. It is famous as a place to observe wild animals as they come to drink at night in the nearby pool; and it is also the place from which Queen Elizabeth was summoned to London on the death of her father, George VI.

The Mau Mau

THE MAU MAU TERRORISM of 1952–56 took place not among the remote and wild tribes but among the Kikuyu, the largest and most advanced of the African groups in Kenya. Kikuyu discontent arose from the loss of land to Europeans, the lack of political rights, the great contrast in living standards between Africans and Europeans, the destruction of tribal customs through the spread of Christianity, and other grievances, some real and some imaginary.

Mau Mau (the origin of the term is uncertain) was an anti-European and anti-Christian revolt which resorted to murder and other brutal methods to force loyal Kikuyu to support it in a campaign designed to drive the Europeans from Kenya.

The Mau Mau played upon traditional customs and fears and compelled Africans to take secret oaths to support the movement, bolster-

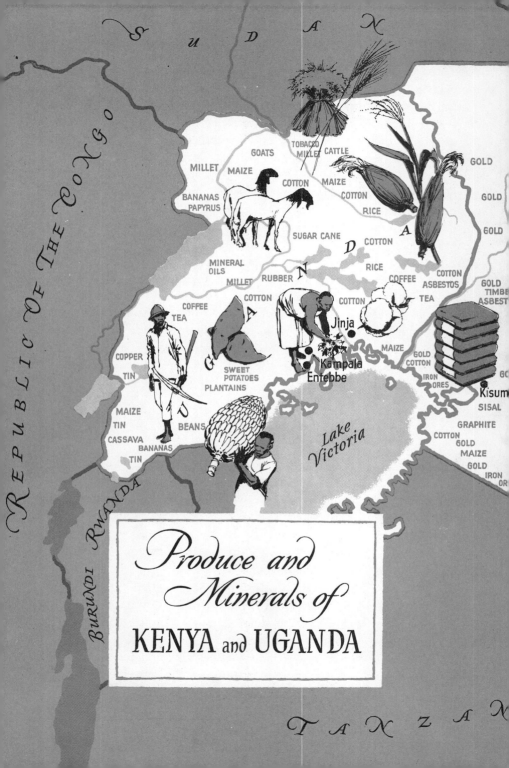

Produce and
Minerals of
KENYA and UGANDA

ing the superstitious power of the oaths with threats of terrible violence. Opposition among the Kikuyu came from those who had accepted Christianity, were aware of the perversion of Kikuyu oaths, or rejected murder and terrorism as methods of securing reforms.

Anti-Mau Mau measures, such as the arming of Europeans and the use of troops, prevented the terrorists from making much progress in killing off the European settlers. In all, only a few dozen of them were murdered. But thousands of Mau Mau and loyal Africans were killed in raids and bush warfare.

For a while, European housewives in the farm regions carried revolvers while they did their housework or went visiting. Meanwhile police, British troops, and European and African volunteers sought out Mau Mau forces in the forests of Mount Kenya and the Aberdares, and screened African employees in Nairobi and the Kikuyu country to find Mau Mau leaders or supporters. By the end of 1956 the revolt had been broken, although a few die-hard terrorists hid out in remote places for many months longer.

HOUSES AND GRAIN STORAGE HUTS IN A NEW KIKUYU VILLAGE

The loyal Kikuyu people (Kenya) were moved into large new villages during the Emergency so that they could be protected against Mau Mau terrorists. The villages have neat rows of huts and granaries.

The New Look in Kikuyuland

BEFORE THE MAU MAU TROUBLES, almost all the rural Kikuyu lived in remote huts that could be reached only by footpaths. They raised their subsistence crops of corn, bananas and vegetables in small patches of land that were scattered far and wide. Increasing population in the crowded reserves caused over-cropping and soil erosion.

During the Emergency, as the Mau Mau period was called, motor roads were pushed into the Kikuyu reserve to permit the rapid movement of police and military vehicles. In order to protect the loyal Kikuyu from the Mau Mau, the farmers were moved into large new villages which could be defended. Every new village was on a motor

43

A trout-rearing pond at the River Research Station on the Upper Sagana River, Kenya. Fish are raised here from eggs flown from England, then studied to discover their reactions to Kenya rivers. Later the trout are used for stocking fishing streams.

Breeding underwater insect life of the trout rivers at the River Research Station in Kenya. The tiers of plates contain gravel from the rivers and specimens of underwater life. Water drips from the pail and from each plate to provide necessary aeration.

road. Many of the old scattered huts were destroyed to deprive the Mau Mau of hiding places. Almost a million people were moved, and the land was changed from one of trails and isolated huts to one of motor roads and accessible large villages.

A scheme to control soil erosion and to consolidate the scattered fragments of land into individual farms was also carried forward. The hilly country was terraced and re-divided among the farmers so that most now have a terraced farm of several acres, instead of three to ten scattered bits of land that totalled the same acreage. Commercial crops such as coffee and tea were also introduced to provide cash incomes.

Schools were rare in Kikuyuland before the Emergency. Now every village has one.

Political changes were also made in Kenya after the Emergency. For the first time, a few Africans were elected to the Kenya Legislature Council to join the Europeans. But the Africans, encouraged by the great swing toward self-government and independence all over the continent, insisted upon a share in government that would be more in proportion to their numbers. Crisis followed crisis until, in 1960, a conference of Kenya representatives of all races met in London and established a new constitution. Since then, in a succession of steps, Kenya has become an independent republic, but still within the British Commonwealth. In December 1963 the British Union Jack was replaced by the black, red and green flag of the new state of Kenya. A year later, on the anniversary of independence, Kenya ended the last direct tie with the United Kingdom, becoming a fully independent republic, with its President as head of state.

A Kikuyu home is made of a framework of poles and branches to support the walls of mud. A roof of grass and an outside coat of whitewash complete the hut.

17.   STREET IN A KIKUYU VILLAGE, KENYA

45

Kenya emerged with a government in which Africans have a majority of the elected representatives and a number of ministerial posts. At the same time, the old restrictions which prevented Africans from owning land in the "White Highlands" were removed. Kenya has a "new look" in government and land policy, as well as in the Kikuyu villages.

The Wild Northern Frontier

Beyond Mount Kenya and the Aberdares to the north is an expanse of frontier country half the size of Texas. This semi-desert

South-eastern Uganda is warm and humid with dense forests interspersed with lakes and marshes. The forests shelter wild animals and beautiful birds, and provide timber for the farms and growing towns.

6.   TROPICAL FOREST IN SOUTHERN UGANDA

46

and desert region is closed to visitors, except by permission, and has nomadic tribes almost untouched by European influences. Many of the people, instead of having a typically Negroid appearance, have Hamitic features—straight noses of narrow or moderate width, thin lips, lithe bodies and thin legs. Skin tone varies from light brown to deep black, and the black hair may be either short and curly or moderately long and straight.

One of the tribes of this region, the Samburu, uses camels for crossing the barren scrublands, and sometimes erects sheets of cloth to provide shelter from the blazing sun. The sheets look like sails, and a string of camels like true "ships of the desert". Samburu men are traditionally trained as warriors and many now join the Kenya Army where they have an outstanding record as fighting men. The steppes and scrubby woods of the Samburu country support cattle, sheep and goats, and the sale of livestock is the major source of income.

The Turkana people graze cattle near Lake Rudolf. And to the north-east of the Samburu are the Boran and Somali nomads. Raids and clashes among these people, and with tribes across the border in Ethiopia, occur over the theft of animals or for revenge for past insults. This is still wild country.

The Kabaka, or King, of Buganda, has his palace and other government buildings at Mengo, adjoining Kampala. The kingdom of Buganda has a parliament (Lukiko) with a Prime Minister.

28.   REED FENCE OF THE KABAKA'S PALACE

Graves of three kings, the ancestors of the present Kabaka of Buganda, are located in a large hut near Kampala, and surviving widows keep a daily vigil at the shrine. Many decades ago human sacrifices were held here by the cruel and unstable Kabaka Mwanga.

Buganda and Uganda

THE FIRST EUROPEAN VISITORS to the north-western shores of Lake Victoria, in 1875, were impressed by the advanced state of the Kingdom of Buganda. There were roads as wide as those in England. The Kabaka, or king, had a capital and court with many huts near the site of present-day Kampala. The people were familiar with government administration, and adopted new ideas more rapidly than any other people in East Africa. The Kabaka accepted Christianity at an early date and spread it among the people.

The name "Uganda" was adapted from "Buganda" and applied to the whole British protectorate, including many areas besides the Kingdom of Buganda. The British found the people from Buganda helpful in administering other areas, and this skill, plus the size of Buganda, about 16,000 square miles, with a population of nearly 2 million, and its head start in economic and political development, have made Buganda the dominant region of Uganda.

The rolling, humid, and fertile lands of Buganda support numerous African farmers who raise cotton and coffee for sale, and bananas and vegetables for food. Small shambas of a few acres produce enough to make their owners prosperous by African standards. Almost all have bicycles, and many have radios and cars. Farmers in Buganda often hire Africans from other areas to do manual work for them. A modern home generally has a corrugated iron roof, plastered walls, a door and windows, and a concrete floor.

Some of the coffee from Uganda is shipped across Lake Victoria to the port of Kisumu, Kenya, to continue by rail to Mombasa for export. The Robusta coffee of Uganda, less expensive than Kenya's highland Arabica coffee, competes with cotton as Uganda's leading export.

Uganda was at first administered in paternalistic fashion, but later moved toward responsible government, with a Legislative Council as a law-making body of limited powers under a British governor. More recently the Africans, as elsewhere, demanded a greater voice in the government. Following a period of planning and negotiation, Uganda, in October, 1962, though remaining within the Commonwealth, became an independent nation.

Economic progress in Uganda is being pushed by plans for developing new industries based upon power from the River Nile, the processing of minerals and agricultural produce, and the manufacture of goods for which there is an assured local market.

49

Kampala and Entebbe

THE LARGEST TOWN and the capital of Uganda are both in Buganda. Kampala has grown up near the Kabaka's capital and now spreads over the green hills for several miles. The population is about 50,000, including the many people clustered in African villages on the margins of the town itself. Most of the stores in the town are Asian, with a few large European enterprises, and a number of small African ones. Kampala is the economic heart of Uganda, and has hard-surfaced roads radiating to many parts of the country.

Buses serve the major cities of Uganda, over the best roads in East Africa. Tarmac highways radiate outward from Kampala for dozens of miles and are continued by maintained gravel or clay roads which reach the secondary towns and are usable at all seasons.

13. STEAMER AT PORT BELL NEAR KAMPALA

Lake steamers make a circuit of Lake Victoria, exchanging goods and passengers among Kenya, Uganda and Tanzania. Port Bell, only five miles from Kampala, serves the densely populated heart of Uganda.

Bright and shining mosques have been built by Moslem communities in all the towns of East Africa. Their domes and minarets give an oriental aspect to some of the larger cities.

2.   MOSLEM MOSQUE IN KAMPALA, UGANDA

Makerere College, the University College of East Africa, with 1,200 students, is located at Kampala and draws African students, plus a modest number of Asians and a few rare Europeans, from all over East Africa.

Entebbe, the capital of Uganda, is located on a peninsula in Lake Victoria some twenty miles south of Kampala. It was built to serve as an administrative city, with wide streets, gardens and government offices, but it has little commerce. The population is about 18,000.

When flying boats were in style, the planes landed on the lake beside Entebbe and the town became a major stop on the route that followed the Nile and the Great Lakes from Egypt to South Africa. Entebbe kept up with the times by building a large airport and now rivals Nairobi as a focus of international air traffic in East Africa. There are also local lines from Entebbe to other towns in Uganda, Kenya and Tanzania.

25.   MAIN BUILDING OF THE UNIVERSITY COLLEGE AT NAIROBI

The University College has a beautiful building with modern equipment. It was established in 1956 to provide the first years of college training for students of all races.

Harnessing the Nile

LAKE VICTORIA, one of the sources of the Nile, lies on the Equator, receives about fifty inches of rain a year, and continually overflows to the north through an outlet known as the Victoria Nile. Until recently the river plunged over the Ripon Falls right at the edge of the lake and, a few miles farther downstream, over the Owen Falls. For decades the idea of harnessing the Nile by building a hydro-electric power dam at the falls had captured the imagination of visitors to Uganda, one of whom, Winston Churchill, advocated such a scheme in his book *My African Journey,* published in 1908. Finally, in 1954, the great Owen Falls Dam was completed at the lowest cascade. It holds back the water so that both Owen Falls and Ripon Falls are now submerged.

Power generated from the hydro-electric station at the dam, which has a capacity of 150,000 kilowatts, will soon be doubled by a supplemental installation about four miles downstream. From the dam area a net of transmission lines covers more than 3,000 miles, taking electricity eastward to Nairobi, westward to Kampala, and northward to several other towns. And at the dam, Jinja has grown from a village to a town.

Fishing in the Victoria Nile below the Owen Falls Dam at Jinja, Uganda. The main highway from Kenya to Uganda runs across the dam and provides visitors with a view of both the river and of the rising industries along its banks.

The Owen Falls Dam provides power at the source of the Nile, and cheap electricity is transforming Jinja into an industrial town. Power generated at the dam is transmitted as far as Nairobi, over 400 miles away.

24.　　THE OWEN FALLS DAM AT JINJA

53

With 30,000 people, it ranks as the second largest town in Uganda. Power from the dam has made it possible to start new industries which process the raw materials of Uganda. Cement, beer, flour, sugar and textiles are typical products.

Beyond the dam the Victoria Nile continues northward over additional cataracts and then pours into shallow and sprawling Lake Kyoga. At the north-western edge of Kyoga the Nile starts peacefully westward and then rushes through fifty miles of rapids that end in the mighty Murchison Falls.

Paraa Safari Lodge overlooks the Nile a short distance below Murchison Falls. A launch carries tourists through waters where hippos and crocodiles abound in unbelievable numbers to the foot of the thundering waterfall.

18.   LODGE AT MURCHISON FALLS PARK

Murchison Falls

A T MURCHISON FALLS the Nile is squeezed into a canyon that is only nineteen feet wide at one point. The stream plunging down into the western Rift Valley in a series of turbulent cascades is one of the most spectacular sights in Africa.

Visitors come from all over the world to see the falls and the abundant wild animals in Murchison Falls National Park. One can drive to an observation point at the top of the falls, or approach them from below, where the river flows calmly for sixteen miles to join Lake Albert. Excursion boats start well below the falls and run up the Nile, past an unbelievable number of crocodiles and hippos, to the base of the falls.

The Nile continues northward through an outlet at the northern end of Lake Albert, where it becomes the White Nile. By using river boats on navigable sections, and motor or rail transport around unnavigable ones, one can go down the Nile from Lake Albert across Uganda, Sudan and Egypt to the Mediterranean Sea, a distance of nearly 3,500 miles.

Mount Elgon and South-eastern Uganda

EAST OF THE NILE and Lake Kyoga, the land slopes gradually upward toward Kenya until, right at the border, the massive extinct volcano of Mount Elgon rises far above the surrounding country. Elgon is fifty miles in diameter at the base and reaches a height of over 14,000 feet. Africans raise coffee on the fertile volcanic soils of the lower slopes; the higher ones are covered with forest.

Asian shops offer a wide variety of goods and are found in every town of Kenya and Uganda. Some Asians have built their concerns from small shops into department stores or chains of shops.

27.   ASIAN STORE IN VOI, KENYA

55

A warrior of Karamoja, north-eastern Uganda, on the way to the market at Kangole to sell cattle. The proud Karamojong men have resisted Western customs such as wearing clothes. They often go nude and carry only a spear and a small wooden headrest.

To the west of Mount Elgon is Mbale, with a population of 13,600, a bright and growing farming town. Farther south is Tororo, at the base of a mass of rock that juts up sharply for hundreds of feet like a giant pedestal. Tororo has phosphates nearby and several industries powered by Owen Falls electricity, including a large cement factory and one engaged in the manufacture of asbestos products.

The densely populated country from Mbale and Tororo to Jinja, in the Eastern Province, is one of the best agricultural areas of East Africa and there are a number of tribes noted for their productive farms. Some of the farmers, with their plots of coffee, cotton, bananas and sugar cane, are even more prosperous than those in Buganda.

No Clothing Needed

A HUNDRED MILES to the north of Mount Elgon the country is much drier and is thinly populated by primitive and semi-nomadic tribes. The Karamojong, as the people of Karamoja are called, are of mixed origin with Hamitic strains predominating. The staple diet, as with the Masai and some of the northern Kenya tribes, is milk mixed with blood. The men often wear as little as a few strings of beads or a headdress of ostrich plumes. Most of them carry spears and tend their cattle in the same manner as in centuries past. Although the Karamojong are a friendly lot under normal conditions, there are still cases of cattle raids and inter-tribal fighting. Visitors cannot enter the district without special permission.

West of Karamoja there are other cattle-raising people, but they have had more contact with the outside world. Also, their country is more humid, with tall grass and scattered woods, instead of dry scrub and sparse grass. Lira and Gulu, on the main road from Mbale northwestward to Sudan, are noted as cattle markets.

12.   CLOCK TOWER AND TRAFFIC CIRCLE ON ENTEBBE ROAD IN KAMPALA

Traffic circles, new buildings, and winding tree-bordered residential streets give Kampala, Uganda, a surprisingly modern and Western appearance. Lawns and trees are lush and green at all seasons.

57

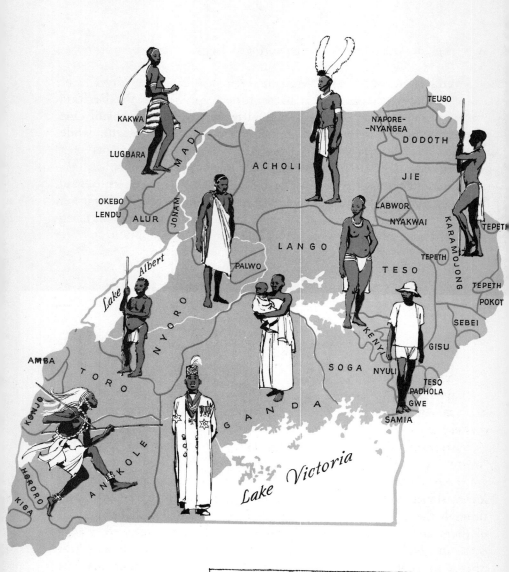

KAKWA
LUGBARA
MADI
OKEBO
LENDU
ALUR
JONAM
NYORO
Lake Albert
AMBA
TORO
KONJO
MORORO
KIGA
ANKOLE
GANDA
PALWO
ACHOLI
LANGO
PADHOLA
TEUSO
NAPORE-
-NYANGEA
DODOTH
JIE
LABWOR
NYAKWAI
KARAMOJONG
TEPETH
TESO
TEPETH
TEPETH
POKOT
SEBEI
GISU
KENYI
SOGA
NYULI
TESO
PADHOLA
GWE
SAMIA
Lake Victoria

Peoples of

UGANDA

Bunyoro

A T THE TIME WHEN THE BRITISH came to Uganda, the Kingdom of Bunyoro was a rival of Buganda. But the rulers of the Bunyoro chose to fight the Europeans rather than make treaties with them. One result was that Buganda gained in area and political strength, while Bunyoro lost territory and was only slowly given a part in its own administration.

Bunyoro is located to the east of Lake Albert and to the north-west of Buganda. The southern part of Murchison Falls National Park lies within it, and there are other areas of magnificent forests and big game. It is one of the best parts of Uganda for elephant hunting.

The people of Bunyoro have the reputation of being friendly and easy-going. Although it has many good farming areas and is noted for tobacco, Bunyoro is not as prosperous as Buganda. Many people drift to Kampala to work as servants, or as farmhands.

The Mountains of the Moon

S INCE THE DAYS of the ancient Romans there have been stories of the legendary "Mountains of the Moon" located somewhere in the heart of Africa. But these mountains were so remote that they were a mystery to explorers and geographers until a few decades ago.

Ruwenzori, meaning "Rainy Mountains", is the modern name, but "misty" or "cloudy" mountains would be as suitable—the mountains are rarely visible. The famous explorer H. M. Stanley camped on their lower slopes but got no glimpse of the towering snow-clad peaks through the clouds. Only on his second trip in 1889 did he see parts of them and have them investigated. Other explorers followed, among them the Duke of the Abruzzi in 1906, and Captain G. Noel Humphreys in 1926. But climbing is difficult for ground parties, and the cloudy weather impedes air observation and photography. Even the latest expeditions have not been able to explore or map all parts of the Ruwenzori.

The Ruwenzori are the only mountains in Uganda to have permanent snow and glaciers. The range is a rugged, uplifted block, seventy-five miles long and forty miles wide, on the border between Uganda and the Republic of the Congo. There are six mountain masses which have glaciated peaks. Mount Stanley, the highest of them, has two peaks that exceed 16,000 feet. Mountain climbers find the lush vegetation of great interest, but they tread carefully through the lower forests and grasslands to avoid exciting the dangerous herds of elephant and buffalo.

Rubies are rare in British East Africa, and Kenya has only one small mine. The important minerals are carbonate of soda from Magadi in Kenya and copper from the Kilembe mines of Uganda.

8.   ROCKS WITH RUBIES FROM A KENYA MINE

Mining in the Far West

JUST EAST OF RUWENZORI is the Kingdom of Toro, with people similar to those of Bunyoro. Toro has a Mukama (ruler) with a palace near Fort Portal. The land is hilly, with tall elephant grass and scattered forests. There are small farms that produce bananas, coffee and tea.

Fort Portal until recently was noted mainly as a trading and administrative town for western Uganda and as a stopping place for visitors to the Ruwenzori and to Queen Elizabeth National Park. But since the Kilembe copper and cobalt mines have been opened near Kasese, about fifty miles south of Fort Portal, the region is gaining fame for its minerals. The Kilembe mines produce nearly 16,000 tons of blister copper a year, and development is continuing.

A railway has been built westward from Kampala to Kasese to serve this mining area. This latest extension completes the line from Mombasa through Nairobi and Kampala almost to the Republic of the Congo.

Queen Elizabeth National Park

LARGE HERDS OF BUFFALO, troops of elephant and pools filled with hippopotamus are typical sights in Queen Elizabeth National Park, just to the south of Ruwenzori and the Kilembe mines. Herds of water buck are almost everywhere, and antelope and wart hog trot warily away if the visitor approaches too close. With a little searching, lions can be found. The leopards are night prowlers and remain in hiding during the day. Monkeys, chimpanzees, giant forest hogs and wild hunting dogs have their chosen localities. There is a profusion of wild birds, large and small.

The park has the additional attractions of the southern foothills of the Ruwenzori, where there are extinct craters with green lakes, and forests of euphorbia. Lake Edward and Lake George, with their peli-

Queen Elizabeth National Park in south-western Uganda is noted for its herds of elephant, buffalo, antelope, and other wild animals. It also includes the southern end of the Ruwenzori Mountains, Lake Edward, the shores of Lake George, and pools with hippopotamus and many water birds.

cans and fish eagles, and elephants bathing at the shores, provide interesting places for boating—or one can just relax.

Ankole Cattle

ANKOLE IS A KINGDOM in south-western Uganda with a ruler known as the Mugabe and a population divided between the tall, aristocratic Hamitic Bahima and the smaller and darker Bantu Bairu. The Bahima own long-horned cattle that have aroused the wonder of explorers. Instead of having a humped back and short horns like the usual Zebu cattle of East Africa, the Ankole cattle have straight backs and enormous horns that curve outward and upward like the sides of a lyre. The distance between the tips of the great horns may be as much as six feet. A group of these large animals, under a forest-like crown of horns, can often be seen to follow their proud and stately herders, instead of being driven.

The semi-nomadic and conservative Bahima retain their traditional affection for their cattle, and gain status mainly through owning large herds. The lush grasslands around Mbarara, the capital of Ankole, provide much better pasture than the semi-arid cattle areas of north-eastern Uganda or northern Kenya.

Gorilla Country

BEYOND ANKOLE, in the extreme south-western corner of Uganda, is the mountainous region of Kigezi. The Mufumbiro (or Birunga) Range of volcanoes, lying partly in Uganda and partly in the Congo, have a special claim to fame. They are the home of the rare mountain gorilla, which is strictly protected. Mount Muhavura, at 13,547 feet, is another peak to tempt the mountain climber.

Kabale, the administrative town for Kigezi, has an elevation of 6,400 feet and is the highest town in Uganda. Nights are so cool that houses have fireplaces. Kabale is a holiday resort for those who wish to climb mountains, go swimming or boating in nearby Lake Bunyonyi, or penetrate "the Impenetrable Forest" on Mufumbiro for a glimpse of the mountain gorillas.

List of Important Dates

A.D. 77   A Greek from Alexandria published the "Periplus of the Erythraean Sea", (Red Sea) which included a description of Mombasa and the east coast.

A.D. 8th century   Arab colonization of the east coast began.

1498   Vasco da Gama visited the east coast on his way to India.

1505   The Portuguese occupied Mombasa.

1698   The Arabs captured Mombasa from the Portuguese, after a long siege.

1784   The Arabs drove the last of the Portuguese from the central coast of East Africa.

1862   J. H. Speke and J. A. Grant, in search of the source of the Nile, were the first Europeans to enter Uganda.

1872   Sir Samuel Baker, governor-general of Anglo-Egyptian Sudan, suppressed slavery along the upper Nile, and part of Uganda was attached to the Sudan until 1889.

1875   H. M. Stanley visited Uganda and sent appeals to Europe which resulted in the sending of missionaries and the conversion of Buganda to Christianity.

1883   Joseph Thomson was the first European to traverse the Highlands of Kenya.

1885   Bishop Hannington, of the Church Missionary Society, was murdered in Uganda.

1887   Sultan Barghash of Zanzibar granted a concession to the British East African Association (later the Imperial British East Africa Company) over the coast of Kenya.

1890   An Anglo-German agreement placed both Uganda and Kenya in the British sphere of influence.

1895   The British Foreign Office acquired the holdings of the Imperial British East Africa Company and formed the East African Protectorate. Work on the Uganda Railway.

1901   The railway was completed to Kisumu.

1903	The first white settlers, including Lord Delamere, arrived to settle in Kenya. Eastern Uganda, including Kisumu, the Kavirondo Gulf, and the Eastern Highlands, were transferred to Kenya.
1914–18	World War I. Kenya forces invaded German East Africa.
1931	The railway was extended from Nakuru, Kenya, to Kampala, Uganda.
1952	The Mau Mau, a secret society among the Kikuyu tribe, carried on terrorist activities in Kenya.
1953	The Kabaka of Buganda was deposed for refusing to cooperate with the British government of Uganda, but was later restored to his position.
1954	Owen Falls Dam was completed.
1956	Police forces and British troops in Kenya brought the Mau Mau revolt to an end.
1960	Both Kenya and Uganda obtained new constitutions which gave Africans a dominant position in the government.
1962	Uganda became independent nation within the Commonwealth.
1963	Kenya became independent nation within the Commonwealth. Owen Falls hydro-electric station was completed and power distribution to both countries was begun on a large scale.
1964	Kenya became a Republic within the Commonwealth, with the President as head of state. It launched a six-year economic scheme.
1965	The Kindaruma Project was started, to build a dam on the Tana River, a power station, and transmission lines to provide more electric power in Kenya.